Baking with
Tiny Tots

NOTES

Both metric and imperial measurements have been given in all recipes. Use one set of measurements only, and not a mixture of both.

Standard level spoon measurements are used in all recipes.
1 tablespoon = one 15 ml spoon
1 teaspoon = one 5 ml spoon
All eggs used in the recipes are medium.

Ovens should be preheated to the specified temperature – if using a fan-assisted oven, follow the manufacturer's instructions for adjusting the time and the temperature.

This book includes dishes made with nuts and nut derivatives. It is advisable for those with known allergic reactions to nuts and nut derivatives and those who may be potentially vulnerable to these allergies, such as pregnant and nursing mothers, invalids, the elderly, babies and children, to avoid foods made with nuts. It is also prudent to check the labels of pre-prepared ingredients for the possible inclusion of nut derivatives.

Children should be supervised by an adult at all times when cooking or baking. The tasks that can be performed at a particular age or stage in their development will differ from child to child.

While the advice and information in this book are believed to be accurate, neither the author nor the publisher can accept any legal responsibility for any illness sustained while following the advice in this book.

First published in Great Britain in 2007 by
Hamlyn, a division of Octopus Publishing Group Ltd
2–4 Heron Quays, London E14 4JP

Copyright © Octopus Publishing Group Ltd 2007

ISBN-13: 978-0-600-61607-8
ISBN-10: 0-600-61607-X

A CIP catalogue record for this book is available from the British Library

Printed and bound in China

10 9 8 7 6 5 4 3 2 1

Becky Johnson

Baking with Tiny Tots

Over 50 easy recipes for young children to enjoy making

hamlyn

Contents

Introduction

Whoever said never to work with children or animals has obviously not tried baking with little ones as it is a joy to cook with even the tiniest of tots. OK, so it may get a little messy but the results are worth it. Children's energy and enthusiasm for cooking are an inspiration, and any doubts that some of the trickier tasks like piping, kneading or rubbing in are beyond their young years are often dispelled by displays of earnest concentration, determination and exuberant completion of the task in hand. That they are then able to eat the results of their labour is invariably met with wonder and joy.

Children like to feel that they contribute to family life. They want to be helpful and do what they see you doing. Baking is one way that they can produce real results, ones that everyone can enjoy and appreciate.

My seven-year-old daughter is genuinely excited by other people's birthdays now as she insists on making them a cake. This is always received with rapturous delight, making her rightly proud.

This book is full of child-friendly ideas for food that you and your little ones can bake together, and all the recipes have been tested on children. A family baking session is a lovely way to spend time together. In this book you'll find ideas for a quick lunch or a teatime cake through to edible Christmas decorations and party treats. Together you can make the food for a picnic or their lunch box, delicious gifts for friends and relatives and irresistible snacks for the cookie jar or cake tin.

Additive-free food Baking at home also gives control back to us parents over what our children eat. The kids can still enjoy sweet treats but without the long list of additives most of us know little about and fear may harm their growing bodies. Instead of giving your children a shop-bought cake, open their young minds to the wonderful variety of textures, smells and tastes of home baking. Show them where their food comes from and how they can combine different ingredients to make yummy biscuits, cakes and pastries. With just a little encouragement, a lifelong interest in real food and cooking may easily be sparked at this tender age.

Be relaxed First baking experiences need to be fun. The recipes in this book are easy and quite quick. They don't require long attention spans but be prepared to step in if your child is wavering before completing the whole tray of cookies! I found my daughter was always happy to sit and lick out the bowl, or 'help' with the washing up in a sink full of bubbles, while I finished off the recipe.

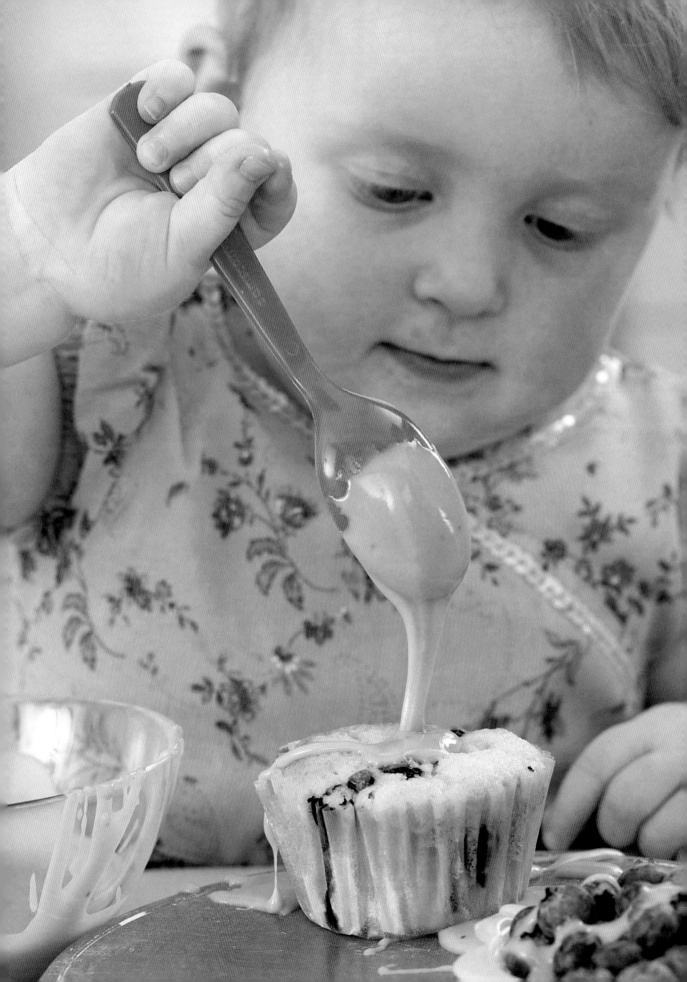

The important thing when cooking with little children is to allow lots of time – children hate being hurried – and not to worry too much about the look of the results! It's the time spent creating something together that's important.

Learning is fun Children learn a huge amount from cooking without even realizing. Firstly, there's the exposure to cookery books full of recipes. From these they learn that the written word provides information that can be used to make things. They also see photos of other children doing things that they will then want to try themselves. Secondly, there's the coordination required to measure out ingredients, to mix, spoon out, beat and spread. Next, weighing and measuring introduce children to the concepts of numbers, weights, volume and accuracy. Lastly, there's the chemistry involved in the baking itself – the transforming effect of heat on food.

Encouraging independence Because cooking is an activity that uses all of the senses, it totally absorbs children. It gives them a sense of achievement and confidence as they try new actions by themselves. As they become older and more capable, your children will be able to make their favourite foods by themselves, and developing a familiarity with food and cooking at a young age may give them the confidence to be more creative in the kitchen in later life.

We live in an age where many people don't know how to cook, and rely heavily on convenience foods and pre-prepared meals. Encouraging your children to cook for themselves and learn how to transform sets of ingredients into cakes, biscuits and eventually casseroles and roast dinners can only be a good thing for them in adulthood and will hopefully encourage them to pass these skills onto their own children in time.

Shopping for ingredients Not only do children learn about food and cooking when in the kitchen, but taking them shopping for the ingredients you're going to use is a learning experience, too. Whether they're sitting in the trolley, or walking along beside you in the supermarket, involve your children in the food shopping process. Teach them how to locate items along the aisles, get them to help you track down specific ingredients and explain their uses and their origin if possible. It all helps spark children's interest and may even encourage fussy eaters to try unfamiliar foods once back at home.

What can your child do? Children can – and indeed like to – help you in the kitchen from the time they are old enough to stand on a chair and reach the worktop. Covering their hands with yours and letting them think they are cutting butter or spreading icing gives them a huge thrill and costs you nothing but patience. Even the smallest child should be able to use a cookie cutter to cut shapes out of dough. Children develop at different rates but between the ages of three and six you'll find they can wash fruits and vegetables for you, stir ingredients in a bowl and, under direction, add ingredients to the bowl. Over-sixes will be able to use measuring spoons, measure liquids into a jug and beat ingredients with a whisk.

> **Recipe steps that young children should find particularly easy to carry out are marked with a chef's hat. Adult supervision is recommended at all times.**

Tips for kneading dough
The best bit of kneading is that it doesn't really need to be done in any specific way so you can throw the dough down on the table and punch it, pull it and twist it. Children are very good at kneading dough, but if they need some instruction, tell them to grab the side of the dough nearest to them and, keeping hold of it, push the other side of the dough down and away from them with the palm of their hand. Then lift the far edge up and over into the centre. Now give the dough a quarter turn and knead again as before. Do this for at least 10 minutes or until the dough becomes smooth textured, elastic and no longer sticky. Children can become tired kneading dough, so do be prepared to step in and finish off the job.

Getting started
First choose your recipe, bearing in mind the age and ability of your child. Remember that cooking with a little one takes much longer than cooking on your own, so make sure you have plenty of time to complete the recipe. Collect together all the necessary ingredients and equipment before you start so you can check you've got what you need. It's infuriating to have to abandon a recipe halfway through cooking because you're missing an ingredient you thought you had. It will also cause intense disappointment on the part of your assistant chef!

What you'll need You don't *have* to buy any special equipment in order to bake with children but certain items will make life easier for them so may mean they enjoy the baking experience more.

- **step-up stool** It's worth investing in a child's step-up stool or a child-sized chair so that your child can see above the worktop and/or have a low table that they can work on. Alternatively they could sit on a clean floor or on a plastic sheet or tablecloth.

- **apron** A little apron is a treat for small cooks. A wipe-clean one will make it particularly easy to avoid splashes and keep your little one clean. A cheaper alternative is to use an old shirt (check out the charity shop) or even a raincoat!

- **digital weighing scales** These are the easiest type of scales for children to use as the figures are clear and easy to read, and it's easier for children to match them exactly to what's given in the recipe book.

- **small wooden spoon** A child-friendly-sized wooden spoon makes beating and mixing much easier for very little ones.

- **a set of measuring spoons** These are useful for accurately measuring ingredients in whole and fractions of teaspoons and tablespoons. Fill the spoons level – a rounded measure could almost double the amount of ingredient required! Don't use everyday spoons as their designs, depths and shapes vary.

- **plastic measuring jugs and bowls** Plastic equipment is obviously better than glass for children's use, in case of clumsy hands.

Safety first Small children must always be supervised in the kitchen. Teach them basic hygiene rules from an early age, as well as telling them about the potential dangers posed by hot ovens, full saucepans and sharp knives.

- **hygiene** Always wash hands before starting to cook and make sure surfaces are clean. Tie back long hair and don an apron or coverall.

- **ovens and hobs** Take special care when opening oven doors in front of expectant little ones and make sure they stand well back so they don't get blasted by very hot air. Always use oven gloves. Also be especially wary of recently turned off but still very hot hobs. Use the back rings of the hob when working with small children so there's no temptation to grab saucepan handles from below to see what's cooking.

- **sharp knives** It's great to involve young children in the clearing-up process – to them it's just as much fun as the cooking and you can establish good working practices from the start. But make it a rule never to place any sharp knives or food processor blades in the sink, where they can easily be hidden by soap bubbles. Instead, rinse them as you go and place them straight back on to the knife rack or into a drawer, well out of harm's way.

Storage If you don't eat them all within hours of baking them, most of the cakes and biscuits in this book will keep for 2–3 days in an airtight container, such as a cake tin or cookie jar. If you want to prepare in advance or decide you only want to finish off half the quantity you have made, un-iced cakes and uncooked biscuit dough can be placed in plastic food storage bags and frozen for up to a month.

1

A piece of cake

Lemon sandcastles

Makes 6
Preparation time 15 minutes
Cooking time 20 minutes

Equipment
6 dariole moulds (or 6-hole muffin tin) •
nonstick baking paper • **pencil** • **scissors**
• **kitchen paper** • **large mixing bowl** •
wooden spoon • **small mixing bowl** •
seive • **dessertspoon** • **baking sheet** •
knife • **cooling rack** • **teaspoon**

Ingredients
100 g (3½ oz) butter or margarine,
    softened, plus extra for greasing
100 g (3½ oz) caster sugar
2 eggs
50 g (2 oz) polenta (ordinary or quick-
    cook variety)
125 g (4 oz) self-raising flour
grated rind of a lemon
2 tablespoons natural yogurt

For the icing
200 g (7 oz) icing sugar, sifted
juice of ½ an unwaxed lemon
pinch of saffron (strands or powdered)
    soaked in 1 tablespoon boiling water
flags, sweets or cake decorations

Planted with cocktail stick flags, these little lemon cakes look like sandcastles and even have an authentic 'gritty' texture from the polenta.

What to do

1   Set the oven to 180°C (350°F), Gas Mark 4. To line the bottom of the dariole moulds, place them on a piece of nonstick baking paper and allow your child to draw around them with a pencil. Then, if the little hands have mastered scissors, cut around the circles and place one in the bottom of each mould.

2   Using kitchen paper, smear some butter or margarine around the sides of the moulds so that the cakes won't stick. If you don't have dariole moulds, use a muffin tray and prepare the same way.

3   After helping you measure out the butter or margarine and the sugar into a large mixing bowl, let your child mix them together with a wooden spoon until really creamy.

4   Break the eggs carefully into a small bowl and add them to the large bowl one at a time, stirring in well. Finally, sift in the flour, add all the other ingredients and stir together until you have a smooth mixture.

5   Help your child to use a dessertspoon to spoon the mixture into the prepared tins until they are about two-thirds full.

6   Place all the moulds together on a baking sheet and bake for 20 minutes, or until golden on top.

7   Slide a knife around the edge of the tins to loosen the cakes and then tip on to a cooling rack and leave until cool.

8   Meanwhile your child can stir together the ingredients to make the icing. Drizzle over the cakes with a teaspoon then decorate with flags, sweets or cake decorations.

Yummy stars

Dark, moist gingerbread cut into stars and drizzled with a bright white glacé icing and sugar stars or silver baubles.

What to do

1. Place the baking tin on a sheet of baking paper and have your child draw around it with a pencil.

2. Cut out the square and place it in the bottom of the tin. Set the oven to 150°C (300°F), Gas Mark 2. Put the treacle in a small saucepan and heat gently.

3. Put the butter and sugar in the large mixing bowl and help your child to beat them together until creamy.

4. Add the treacle and egg and stir to combine. Sift in the flour and ginger and stir in. Scrape into the prepared tin and bake for 30 minutes or until a skewer inserted in the middle comes out clean.

5. Leave the cake in the tin to cool and then tip out and, using a star cutter, help your child to cut the cake into 15 star shapes. Eat the trimmings!

6. Meanwhile, make the icing by stirring together the ingredients in a small bowl. Drizzle the icing over the stars with a teaspoon and then decorate with silver baubles.

Makes 15 stars
Preparation time 20 minutes
Cooking time 30 minutes

Equipment
large baking tin, 30 cm (12 inches) square • nonstick baking paper • pencil scissors • small saucepan • large mixing bowl • wooden spoon • seive • spatula • thin wooden or metal skewer • star-shaped cutter • dessertspoon • small mixing bowl • teaspoon

Ingredients
1 tablespoon black treacle
150 g (5 oz) butter or margarine, softened
150 g (5 oz) dark brown sugar
1 egg
300 g (10 oz) self-raising flour
2 teaspoons ground ginger
150 ml (¼ pint) natural yogurt

For the icing
1 tablespoon lemon juice (or water)
200 g (7 oz) icing sugar, sifted
1 tablespoon warm water
edible silver baubles, to decorate

Rock buns

Makes 12
Preparation time 15 minutes
Cooking time 15–20 minutes

Equipment
2 large baking sheets • nonstick baking paper • scissors • large mixing bowl • seive • wooden spoon • dessertspoon • cooling rack

Ingredients
100 g (3½ oz) butter, softened
225 g (7½ oz) self-raising flour
½ teaspoon cinnamon (optional)
grated rind of an orange
100 g (3½ oz) demerara sugar, plus extra for sprinkling
100 g (3½ oz) mixed dried fruit (if your child is not keen on the shop-bought mixes, you can make your own version by chopping dried apricots, glacé cherries and citrus peel)
1 egg, beaten
drop of milk (optional)

Contrary to their name, these little buns are soft and sweet, but they do look rather like rugged rocks.

What to do

1   Help your child to cut large pieces of the baking paper to fit the baking sheets while you set the oven to 200°C (400°F), Gas Mark 6.

2   Put the butter into a large bowl, sift in the flour and cinnamon, if using, and tell your child to put their hands in the bowl and rub the flour and butter together until the butter is all broken up and covered in flour and the mixture resembles breadcrumbs.

3   Add the orange rind, sugar, fruit and egg and stir it all together with a wooden spoon (this stage is too sticky for hands to manage). Add a little milk if the mixture is too crumbly.

4   Use a dessertspoon to put untidy mounds of the mixture on to the baking sheets.

5   Sprinkle the tops of the buns with a little more demerara sugar, then bake for 15–20 minutes or until golden brown on the edges.

6   Remove from the oven and allow to cool for 15 minutes on the tray, then transfer to a cooling rack.

Blueberry and apple muffins

Quick and easy, these ingredients could be measured out, placed in two separate bowls the night before then put together and baked for a special breakfast – a Mother's Day treat perhaps.

What to do

 1   Show your child how to put the paper cases into the muffin tin while you set the oven to 200°C (400°F), Gas Mark 6.

2   Divide the ingredients into two large mixing bowls: all the dry ingredients (sifted flour, bicarbonate of soda and sugar) in one bowl and all the wet (melted butter, yogurt, milk, egg, blueberries and apple) in another.

3   Ask your child to stir the ingredients in their separate bowls until well mixed.

4   Help your child pour the wet ingredients into the dry. It is important to mix quickly and minimally – as with all muffins, it's best to have a lumpy mixture that will be soft and rise rather than a well-mixed one that will not rise and be tough.

5   Quickly spoon the mixture into the prepared cases so that each is about three-quarters full. Have your child sprinkle each with a little more of the sugar. Bake for 20 minutes or until risen and golden.

6   Remove the muffins from the oven and let them cool a little in the tin before transferring to a cooling rack. Eat warm or cold.

Makes 12
Preparation time 15 minutes
Cooking time 20 minutes

Equipment
12 paper muffin cases • 12-cup muffin tin • sieve • 2 large mixing bowls • wooden spoon • dessertspoon • cooling rack

Ingredients
200 g (7 oz) self-raising flour
½ teaspoon bicarbonate of soda
100 g (3½ oz) soft light brown sugar, plus extra for sprinkling
100 g (3½ oz) butter, melted
100 ml (3½ fl oz) natural yogurt
100 ml (3½ fl oz) milk
1 egg, beaten
200 g (7 oz) blueberries
1 dessert apple, cored, peeled and diced quite small

Lamingtons

Makes 12
Preparation time 20 minutes
Cooking time 15–20 minutes

Equipment

**2 x 1 kg (2 lb) loaf tins • nonstick baking
paper • large mixing bowl • wooden
spoon, fork or electric beater • sieve •
cooling rack • medium-sized mixing
bowl • small bowl • saucer • large
serrated knife • palette knife •
board or plate**

Ingredients

**100 g (3½ oz) butter or margarine,
   softened
100 g (3½ oz) caster sugar
2 eggs
200 g (7 oz) self-raising flour
1 teaspoon vanilla essence
about 3 tablespoons milk**

For the icing

**50 g (2 oz) butter or margarine, softened
150 g (5 oz) icing sugar, sifted
1 tablespoon cocoa powder
2–3 tablespoons pre-boiled warm water
50–75 g (2–3 oz) desiccated coconut
1–2 tablespoons milk (optional)**

For the filling

**4 tablespoons raspberry
   or strawberry jam**

As Australian as kangaroos, these jam-filled
sponge cakes taste exceedingly good and are
fun and messy to make!

What to do

1   Set the oven to 180°C (350°F), Gas Mark 4, and grease
    and line the loaf tins with nonstick baking paper.

2   Put the butter and sugar in a large mixing bowl and, using
    a wooden spoon, fork or electric beater, mash them
    together until light and creamy.

3   Beat in the eggs one at a time. Sift in the flour, add the
    vanilla and just enough milk to combine to a soft
    dropping consistency.

4   Spoon into the prepared tins and smooth the top. Bake for
    15–20 minutes or until golden brown and springy to the
    touch. Remove from the tin and cool on a rack.

5   Meanwhile, make the icing. Beat the butter and sugar
    together until light and creamy. In a separate small bowl,
    mix the cocoa and water together and then add to the
    butter mix and beat until smooth.

6   Tip the desiccated coconut into a saucer. Slice the cakes in
    half crossways through the middle and spread the bases
    with jam. Replace the tops and cut each cake into
    6 equal-sized squares.

7   Dip all sides of the squares first into the chocolate icing
    and then into the coconut. Set on to a board or plate to
    dry completely before serving (if towards the end the icing
    becomes too thick, simply thin it down with a spoonful or
    two of milk).

Banana muffins

A great recipe for little ones to make as the secret to a good muffin is not to mix it too well. Lumpy is good!

What to do

1 Ask your child to place the paper cases in the tin while you set the oven to 180°C (350°F), Gas Mark 4.

2 Put the butter, honey and milk in the small pan and place on a low heat until melted.

3 Show your child how to mash the bananas with a fork in the small bowl. Sift the flour and bicarbonate of soda into a large bowl and mix together.

4 Pour the melted butter mixture into the mashed bananas and mix, then tip into the flour and mix together with a wooden spoon. At this stage tell your child not to over-mix – just a couple of stirs will do or the muffins will be tough and flat.

5 Without delay, spoon the mixture into the muffin cases so that each is about two-thirds full. Bake for 20–25 minutes, until risen and golden.

6 Remove from the oven and allow to cool in the tin for 5 minutes, then transfer the muffins in their cases to a cooling rack.

7 While the muffins are cooling, make the caramel icing. Sift the icing sugar into a bowl, add the caramel sauce and mix together with enough pre-boiled warm water, about 2–3 tablespoons, to make a thick but spoonable icing. When cool, ask your child to blob the icing on top of each muffin with a teaspoon and let it run. Stick a banana chip to the wet icing to decorate.

Makes 6
Preparation time 15 minutes
Cooking time 20–25 minutes

Equipment
6 paper muffin cases • **6-cup muffin tin** • **small saucepan** • **fork** • **small mixing bowl** • **sieve** • **large mixing bowl** • **wooden spoon** • **dessertspoon** • **cooling rack** • **teaspoon**

Ingredients
25 g (1 oz) butter
2 tablespoons runny honey
2 tablespoons milk
2 large very ripe bananas
150 g (5 oz) self-raising flour
½ teaspoon bicarbonate of soda

For the icing
175 g (6 oz) icing sugar
1 teaspoon caramel sauce
2–3 tablespoons preboiled warm water
dried banana chips, to decorate

Rainbow buns

These little orange-scented buns are iced and dipped in hundreds and thousands.

What to do

1. Show your child how to place the cake cases in the patty tin while you set the oven to 180°C (350°F), Gas Mark 4.

2. Put the butter, sugar, orange rind and vanilla essence into the mixing bowl and help your child beat them together until creamy.

3. Add the egg and beat the mixture again, then sift in the flour and stir it in. Spoon the mixture into the cake cases with a teaspoon so they are three-quarters full.

4. Bake the buns for 10–15 minutes or until they are risen and golden. Remove from the oven and allow to cool for a few minutes before transferring to a cooling rack and letting them cool completely.

5. Meanwhile, make the icing by sifting the icing sugar into a bowl and stirring it together with the orange juice.

6. When the cakes are cool, drizzle the icing over them with a teaspoon or dip them into the icing to cover. Pour the hundreds and thousands into a saucer and dip in the iced cakes. Leave to set.

Makes 24 mini cakes or 12 cup cakes
Preparation time 20 minutes
Cooking time 10–15 minutes

Equipment
**24 small cake cases or 12 cup cake cases
• 24- or 12-cup patty tin • large mixing
bowl • wooden spoon • sieve •
teaspoon • cooling rack • saucer**

Ingredients
**50 g (2 oz) butter or margarine, softened
50 g (2 oz) caster sugar
grated rind of an unwaxed orange
few drops vanilla essence
1 egg
50 g (2 oz) self-raising flour**

For the icing
**175 g (6 oz) icing sugar
2 tablespoons orange juice
hundreds and thousands or other cake
   decorations**

Flower fairy cakes

Makes 12
Preparation time 10 minutes
Cooking time 15–20 minutes

Equipment
**12 paper muffin cases • 12-cup muffin tin
food processor (or mixing bowl and
wooden spoon) • dessertspoon • cooling
rack • sharp knife • small bowls for
colouring the icing • teaspoons**

Ingredients
**125 g (4 oz) butter or margarine,
  softened
125 g (4 oz) caster sugar
2 eggs
125 g (4 oz) self-raising flour
few drops vanilla essence
2 tablespoons milk**

For the icing
**500 g (1 lb) pack instant royal icing
food colouring (one or more colours,
  as desired)
sugar or rice paper flowers or other cake
  decorations**

Children love to ice and decorate these pretty,
light-as-fairies buns.

What to do

1 Ask your child to put the paper cases in the muffin tin
while you set the oven to 180°C (350°F), Gas Mark 4.

2 If you have a food processor, put all the ingredients except
the milk into it and mix until smooth, then add the milk a
little at a time down the funnel of the food processor until
you have a mixture that is a soft, dropping consistency.
Alternatively, follow steps 2–3 of the Lamington recipe on
page 22 for the manual method.

3 Help your child to spoon mixture into the cases.

4 Bake cakes for 15–20 minutes or until they are golden and
springy to the touch. Allow to cool for a few minutes in
the tin, then transfer to a cooling rack. When cool, slice
off the pointy tops with a sharp knife.

5 Make up the royal icing as directed on the pack and then
divide into small bowls, one for each choice of colour.

6 To colour the royal icing, first cover any porous work
surface with a plastic cloth or newspaper, or work on a
metal draining board. Pour a few drops of colouring into
the lid of the bottle, then ask your child to add the
colouring to the first bowl of icing drop by drop. Add
different colouring to the other bowls of icing if you like.

7 Mix the icing well and let your child spoon the icing on to
the cakes and decorate to their taste.

Coconut and raspberry cup cakes

Makes 12
Preparation time 15 minutes
Cooking time 20 minutes

Equipment
**12 paper muffin cases • 12-cup muffin tin
• small saucepan • large mixing bowl •
wooden spoon • large measuring jug •
cooling rack**

Ingredients
**125 g (4 oz) butter
50 g (2 oz) desiccated coconut
200 g (7 oz) icing sugar
75 g (3 oz) self-raising flour
4 egg whites
200 g (7 oz) fresh raspberries**

These delicious cup cakes are studded with clusters of fresh raspberries.

What to do

1   Show your child how to place the paper cases in the muffin tin while you set the oven to 180°C (350°F), Gas Mark 4.

2   Put the butter in a small saucepan and melt over a low heat. Meanwhile, help your child to sift the flour and icing sugar into a large mixing bowl, add the coconut and stir together.

3   Add the egg whites and stir together, then add the melted butter and stir again until combined into a thick batter.

4   Tip the batter into a measuring jug and help your child pour the batter into the prepared muffin cases, filling each one about half full.

5   Ask you child to place a few raspberries on the top of each cake.

6   Bake the cakes for 20 minutes or until they are golden and springy to the touch. Remove them from the oven and allow to cool for a few minutes in the tin before transferring them to a cooling rack.

Mud pies

This recipe is a little bit tricky in that it needs a lot of whisking, but it's worth the effort for the rich, gooey mud mixture and resulting irresistible pies.

Makes 12
Preparation time 20 minutes
Cooking time 15 minutes

Equipment
12-cup muffin tin • 12 paper muffin cases • small saucepan • medium heatproof bowl • large mixing bowl, preferably with a pouring lip • hand-held electric whisk (or food processor with whisk attachment) • sieve • large metal spoon • cooling rack • tea strainer or small sieve

Ingredients
200 g (7 oz) dark chocolate, broken into small pieces
200 g (7 oz) butter
3 eggs
75 g (3 oz) caster sugar
100 g (3½ oz) self-raising flour
2 tablespoons cocoa powder or icing sugar to decorate (optional)

What to do

 1 Ask your child to put the paper cases in the muffin tin while you set the oven to 160°C (325°F), Gas Mark 3.

2 Boil the kettle and pour 5 cm (2 inches) of water into the small saucepan and set it over a low heat so that the water is simmering.

3 Put the chocolate pieces and butter in the heatproof bowl and place over the simmering water in the saucepan until melted, then stir together gently.

4 Put the eggs and sugar in the large mixing bowl and help your child to beat with the electric whisk for a full 5 minutes, until very light and foamy. Alternatively, this could be done more easily in a food processor with a whisk attachment.

 5 Have your child sift the flour into the egg foam. Add the chocolate mixture and show them how to fold them together with a large metal spoon, being careful not to knock all the air out of the mixture.

6 Help them to pour or spoon the 'mud' into the muffin cases so that each is about half full, then bake for 15 minutes.

7 When they are cooked, remove them from the oven and allow to cool for 5–10 minutes in the tin before transferring them to a cooling rack.

 8 If you wish, your child can put a tablespoon or so of cocoa powder or icing sugar into a tea strainer or small sieve and dust the cakes to decorate.

Chocolate teddies

The easiest one-bowl bun mixture made with dark and white chocolate chips. Here we've decorated them as teddies but let your child use their own decorative ideas.

What to do

1. Show your child how to place the paper cases in the patty tin while you set the oven to 180°C (350°F), Gas Mark 4.

2. Put the butter, sugar and vanilla essence in the mixing bowl and help your child beat them together until creamy.

3. Add the eggs and beat the mixture again, then sift in the flour and stir it in. Finally, stir in the chocolate drops. Spoon the mixture into the cake cases with a dessertspoon so that they are three-quarters full.

4. Bake for 10–15 minutes or until risen and golden. Remove from the oven and allow to cool for a few minutes before transferring to a cooling rack and letting cool completely.

5. Meanwhile, make the chocolate butter icing by sifting the icing sugar and cocoa into a bowl, adding the butter, then beating the ingredients together until smooth.

6. When the cakes are cool, spread them with the icing. Use a fork to make the icing look like fur and then decorate them, making eyes, ears and a nose.

Makes 12
Preparation time 20 minutes
Cooking time 10–15 minutes

Equipment
12 cup cake cases • **12-cup patty tin** • **large mixing bowl** • **wooden spoon** • **dessertspoon** • **cooling rack** • **medium mixing bowl** • **fork**

Ingredients
100 g (3½ oz) butter, softened
100 g (3½ oz) caster sugar
few drops vanilla essence
2 eggs
100 g (3½ oz) self-raising flour
50 g (2 oz) milk chocolate drops
50 g (2 oz) white chocolate drops

For the chocolate icing
50 g (2 oz) butter, softened
150 g (5 oz) icing sugar
2 tablespoons cocoa powder

To decorate
white and milk chocolate buttons/drops

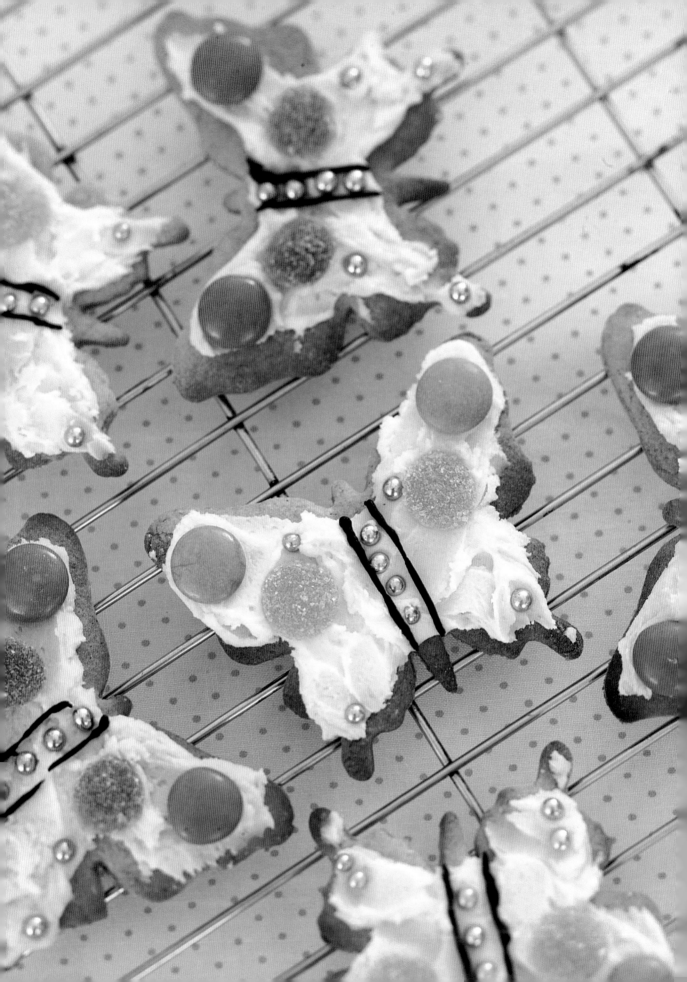

2

Cute cookies

Chocolate chip cookies

These chunky, chocolate-chip-laden cookies are quick, easy and fun to make.

Makes about 24
Preparation time 10 minutes
Cooking time 10–15 minutes

What to do

1   Help your child to cut out two large sheets of baking paper to line the baking sheets while you set the oven to 190°C (375°F), Gas Mark 5.

2   Place the butter and sugar in the mixing bowl and help your child beat them together either with an electric whisk or a wooden spoon until creamy.

3   Add the egg and vanilla essence and mix together again. Place the sieve over the mixing bowl, sift in the flour and then mix in.

4   Add the oats and chocolate drops and stir in, then, using a teaspoon and a finger to scrape the mixture off, place generous spoonfuls of the mixture in 24 or so lumpy heaps on the baking sheets. Allow plenty of space between the heaps as the cookies will spread as they cook.

5   Bake the cookies for about 10 minutes, until the ones on the top shelf are golden brown, then remove them from the oven and move the other baking sheet up from the bottom shelf. Bake these for a further 3–5 minutes until they are golden, then remove.

6   Cool the cookies on the baking sheets for a few minutes before transferring, with a fish slice or palette knife, to a cooling rack. The cookies will crisp up as they cool.

Equipment
nonstick baking paper • scissors • 2 baking sheets • large mixing bowl • hand-held electric whisk or wooden spoon • sieve • teaspoon • fish slice or palette knife • cooling rack

Ingredients
100 g (3½ oz) butter or margarine, softened
100 g (3½ oz) soft light brown sugar
1 egg
1 teaspoon vanilla essence
150 g (5 oz) self-raising flour
75 g (3 oz) porridge oats
50 g (2 oz) plain or milk chocolate drops
50 g (2 oz) white chocolate drops

Coconut racoons

Discs of coconut macaroon with one side dipped in melted chocolate to give them a stripy, racoon look. We like these with vanilla ice cream.

What to do

1 Ask your child to cut out 2 sheets of the baking paper to line the baking sheets while you set the oven to 160°C (325°F), Gas Mark 3.

2 Place the egg whites in a mixing bowl and help your child to use an electric or hand whisk to beat the whites until they form peaks when you turn off (if electric) and lift up the whisk.

3 Add about one-third of the sugar and whisk it in. Add another third and whisk that in, then the final third.

4 Add the coconut and, using a large metal spoon, show your child how to fold it in gently so as not to knock the air out of the mixture.

5 Use a teaspoon to fill an egg cup with the mixture and then tip out mounds on to the baking sheets, leaving a little space between each one.

6 Bake the macaroons for 15 minutes or until the tops are golden brown. Leave to cool on the baking sheets for 2–3 minutes, then remove with a fish slice or palette knife to a cooling rack.

7 Meanwhile, melt the chocolate by placing it in the heatproof bowl over a small saucepan of simmering water. When it has melted, stir the chocolate then remove the bowl from the pan and allow to cool a little.

8 Help your child to dip the cool macaroons into the chocolate and place on fresh pieces of baking paper until set.

9 When set, peel the macaroons off the paper with a palette knife or fish slice.

Makes about 20
Preparation time 15 minutes
Cooking time 15 minutes

Equipment
nonstick baking paper • scissors • 2 large baking sheets • large mixing bowl • hand-held electric whisk or hand whisk • large metal spoon • teaspoon • egg cup • fish slice or palette knife • cooling rack • small heatproof bowl • small saucepan • wooden spoon

Ingredients
3 egg whites
100 g (3½ oz) golden caster sugar
200 g (7 oz) desiccated coconut
100 g (3½ oz) plain chocolate, broken into small pieces, to decorate

Sparkly starfish

Buttery shortbread cut into tiny stars and decorated with sparkly sugar, these little biscuits make great presents stacked into a cellophane bag and tied with a pretty ribbon.

What to do

1   Help your child to cut out 2 large sheets of baking paper to line the baking sheets while you set the oven to 160°C (325°F), Gas Mark 3.

 2   Place the flour, rice flour and sugar in the mixing bowl and have your child mix them together with their hand. Add the butter in one or two big lumps and let your child work it into the dry ingredients with their fingers, squishing and kneading it into a soft dough. (See tips on kneading dough on page 10.)

 3   Add the colouring and squish the dough until the colouring is evenly mixed through and you have a light green dough.

 4   Dust the work surface with flour and place the dough into the middle. Help your child press out the dough with the ball of their hand until it is about 5 mm (¼ inch) thick.

5   Show your child how to use a floured cutter to cut out the shapes, then place them on the prepared baking sheets. Keep squishing the leftover bits of pastry together until you can't cut out any more stars.

6   Brush the shapes with a little egg and then sprinkle with the demerara sugar or cake decorations. Bake for 10 minutes or until golden around the edges.

7   Remove the biscuits from the oven and leave on the baking sheets until cool. Store in an airtight container.

Tiny Tip

Rice flour gives the biscuits a slightly crunchy texture but can be omitted, in which case use 175 g (6 oz) plain flour.

Makes about 100
Preparation time 30 minutes
Cooking time 10 minutes

Equipment
nonstick baking paper • scissors • 2 large baking sheets • mixing bowl • sieve • small star or other shaped cutter • pastry brush

Ingredients
150 g (5 oz) plain flour, plus exra for dusting
3 tablespoons rice flour
50 g (2 oz) caster sugar
100 g (3½ oz) butter, softened
few drops green food colouring
1 small egg, beaten
25 g (1 oz) demerara sugar or coloured sugar cake decorations

Dotty brownies

These fantastically gooey, chewy brownies are dotted with white chocolate.

Makes 16
Preparation time 20 minutes
Cooking time 20 minutes

Equipment
cake tin, 20 cm (8 inches) square · nonstick baking paper · pencil and scissors · small heatproof mixing bowl · small saucepan · large mixing bowl · wooden spoon · sieve · spatula · knife

Ingredients
150 g (5 oz) plain chocolate, broken into small pieces
125 ml (4 fl oz) sunflower, vegetable or peanut oil
200 g (7 oz) soft light brown sugar
2 eggs
75 g (3 oz) self-raising flour
4 tablespoons cocoa powder
50 g (2 oz) white chocolate drops or buttons

What to do

1 Set the oven to 180°C (350°F), Gas Mark 4. Place the cake tin on a piece of baking paper and get your child to draw around it with a pencil. Cut out the square and use it to line the cake tin.

2 Place the chocolate in the small heatproof bowl. Boil a kettle and pour approximately 5 cm (2 inches) of water into the small pan and then place on a low heat.

3 Place the bowl containing the chocolate over this simmering water so that it is suspended on the top of the saucepan and the chocolate will melt slowly.

4 Place the oil, sugar and eggs in the large mixing bowl and ask your child to stir them vigorously with the wooden spoon.

5 When melted, pour the chocolate into the mixture and stir it in.

6 Sift the flour and cocoa powder into the mixture. Mix this in and then pour the mixture into the prepared tin. Help your child to use the spatula to scrape out the bowl so every last bit is used.

7 Ask your child to scatter handfuls of the white chocolate drops over the top of the mixture in the tin.

8 Place the tin on the top shelf of the oven and bake for 20 minutes. The brownies should still be slightly soft in the centre. Leave in the tin to cool then cut into 16 pieces.

Tiny Tip

If you wish, add pieces of walnuts or pecan nuts to the mixture.

Soft and scrummy flapjacks

A soft, buttery oat flapjack made with a splash of apple juice and decorated with chocolate buttons.

Makes 12
Preparation time 15 minutes
Cooking time 20–25 minutes

Equipment
nonstick baking paper • **pencil** •
scissors • **cake tin, 20 cm (8 inches)**
square • **large saucepan** • **wooden**
spoon • **sharp knife** • **palette knife** •
serving plate

Ingredients
150 g (5 oz) butter
75 g (3 oz) soft light brown sugar
75 g (3 oz) golden syrup
50 ml (2 fl oz) apple juice
225 g (7½ oz) porridge oats
50 g (2 oz) white or milk chocolate drops

What to do

1   Set the oven to 180°C (350°F), Gas Mark 4. Take a piece of baking paper and lay it on the work surface, then have your child place the cake tin on top and draw around it with a pencil. Cut out the square of baking paper and use it to line the tin.

2   Help your child measure out the butter, sugar and golden syrup into a large saucepan and then place it on a gentle heat on the hob for them. Stir until the mixture has melted and is just starting to bubble.

3   Remove the pan from the heat and add the apple juice and the oats, then stir together until all the oats are evenly covered. Tip the mixture into the prepared tin and help your child to use the wooden spoon to spread the mixture into the corners and smooth the surface.

4   Ask your child to sprinkle handfuls of the chocolate buttons over the flapjacks.

5   Bake the flapjacks in the oven for 20–25 minutes or until they are a deep golden colour. Be aware that they will still look very soft when they are hot but will set as they cool. Remove from the oven and slice into 12 or so even-sized pieces but leave in the tin to cool completely.

 6   When the flapjacks are cool, ask your child to remove them from the tin with the palette knife and place them on a serving plate.

Crescent moon cookies

Little almond-flavoured soft cookies that are fun to shape.

What to do

1   Show your child how to cut a large sheet of the baking paper to fit the baking sheet while you set the oven to 160°C (325°F), Gas Mark 3.

2   Place the sugar and butter in the mixing bowl and get your child to mash them together vigorously with a wooden spoon, or a hand-held electric whisk if they can manage one, until they are thoroughly mixed and creamy.

3   Add the water and almond essence and stir in. Finally, sieve in the flour and add the ground almonds, then gently stir the mixture together until you have a soft dough.

4   Dip your and your little one's hands in flour to stop the dough sticking. Pick up walnut-sized pieces of the dough and shape into crescents by rolling into sausages with fatter middles and curved ends. Place on the baking sheet.

5   Bake the biscuits for 20–25 minutes or until they are set and golden. Remove from the oven and allow to cool on the baking sheet for 10 minutes then transfer with a fish slice to a cooling rack.

6   When the cookies are completely cool, dust them with icing sugar.

Makes 16
Preparation time 30 minutes
Cooking time 20–25 minutes

Equipment
nonstick baking paper • scissors • baking sheet • large mixing bowl • wooden spoon or hand-held electric whisk • sieve • fish slice • cooling rack

Ingredients
50 g (2 oz) caster sugar
100 g (3½ oz) butter or margarine, softened
1 tablespoon water
1 teaspoon almond essence
150 g (5 oz) plain flour, plus extra for dusting hands
75 g (3 oz) ground almonds
icing sugar for dusting

Marzipan buttons

Little cookies sandwiched with a soft marzipan centre and drizzled with chocolate.

Makes 30
Preparation time 45 minutes
Cooking time 10 minutes

Equipment

nonstick baking paper • scissors • 2 baking sheets • large mixing bowl • hand-held electric whisk or hand whisk • sieve • wooden spoon • knife • small saucepan • small heatproof bowl • cooling rack • teaspoon

Ingredients

200 g (7 oz) butter, softened
200 g (5 oz) soft light brown sugar
1 egg, beaten
1 teaspoon vanilla essence
300 g (10 oz) plain flour, plus extra for dusting hands
200 g (7 oz) marzipan paste
100 g (3½ oz) milk or white chocolate

What to do

1   Ask your child to cut 2 large sheets of the baking paper to fit the baking sheets while you set the oven to 170°C (340°F), Gas Mark 3½.

2   Place the butter and sugar in the mixing bowl. Help your child mix with an electric or hand whisk until the mixture is pale and fluffy. Add the egg and vanilla essence then beat again. Sift in the flour and stir with a wooden spoon.

3   Dip your little one's hand in flour to stop the mixtue sticking. Show your child how to take walnut-sized pieces of the mixture, roll them into balls, then place them on the baking sheets and flatten them slightly into circles.

4   When there are about 30 dough circles (which should use just over half the mixture), cut the marzipan into 30 even-sized pieces and have your child roll these into balls, then put one in the middle of each cookie.

5   Take slightly smaller amounts of the remaining dough mixture and gently flatten on top of the marzipan to sandwich it. Gently press the edges together then place the baking sheets in the oven and bake for 7 minutes.

6   Meanwhile, boil some water in the small saucepan and set the heatproof bowl on top. Break the chocolate into the bowl and allow to melt slowly, then stir until smooth.

7   Remove the cookies from the oven and allow to cool on the baking sheets for a few minutes before transferring to a cooling rack.

8   Use a teaspoon to drizzle the melted chocolate over the cookies to decorate. Cool before serving.

Funny faces

Makes 12
Preparation time 20 minutes
Cooking time 20 minutes

Equipment

**12 paper cake cases • 12-hole patty tin
• large mixing bowl • wooden spoon
or electric hand-held whisk • sieve •
dessertspoon • cooling rack • 2 medium
mixing bowls • teaspoon**

Ingredients

**100 g (3½ oz) butter or margarine,
    softened
100 g (3½ oz) caster sugar
2 eggs
100 g (3½ oz) self-raising flour
3 tablespoons cocoa powder**

For the icing

**75 g (3 oz) butter, softened
175 g (6 oz) icing sugar, sifted
1 tablespoon milk or water
2–3 drops red food colouring and/or
    2 tablespoons cocoa powder**

To decorate

**icing pens
white and milk chocolate buttons
cake decorations**

A very simple cake mix, like butterfly cakes (see page 80), but decorated to make funny faces. They were a big hit at my daughter's school fair and caused an excited rush to the cake stall.

What to do

1   Show your child how to place a paper case in each of the cups in the patty tin while you set the oven to 180°C (350°F), Gas Mark 4.

2   Place the butter and sugar in the mixing bowl and beat together with the wooden spoon or electric whisk until smooth and creamy.

3   Crack the eggs for your child and then have them break them into the mixture one at a time, being careful not to let any shell fall in. Beat the mixture again between egg additions.

4   Place the sieve over the mixing bowl and sift in the flour and cocoa powder, then stir in. Have your child drop dessertspoonfuls of the mixture into the prepared cases.

5   Bake for 20 minutes or until springy to the touch.

6   Remove from the oven and allow to cool in the tin for a few minutes, then transfer to a cooling rack and allow to cool completely.

7   Meanwhile, make the icing. Place the butter, sugar and milk in a bowl and beat together, then divide into two bowls. Add the colouring to one and the cocoa powder to the other. Mix in, then leave them in a cool place.

8   When the cakes are cool, smooth on the butter icing with the back of a teaspoon, then use your imagination to decorate them with lots of different funny faces.

Chilly choc and marshmallow bars

These bars could be made by substituting the marshmallows with nuts (such as pistachios, walnuts or pecans).

Makes 36 bars
Preparation time 15 minutes
Chilling time at least 1 hour

Equipment
**small saucepan • small heatproof bowl •
1 kg (2 lb) loaf tin • nonstick baking paper
• scissors • wooden spoon • clingfilm •
chopping board • sharp knife**

Ingredients
100 g (3½ oz) plain chocolate
100 g (3½ oz) white chocolate
50 g (2 oz) butter
100 ml (3½ fl oz) water
**100 g (3½ oz) digestive or rich tea
   biscuits, broken into small pieces**
50 g (2 oz) mini marshmallows
**50 g (2 oz) golden marzipan, chopped
   into small pieces**

What to do

1 Pour boiling water from the kettle into the small saucepan so that there is about 5 cm (2 inches) in the bottom and set on a low heat.

2 With help from your child, break the chocolate into small pieces and place in the heatproof bowl. Add the butter and water and set this over the simmering water in the pan.

3 While the chocolate melts, help your little one to line the loaf tin by cutting out a piece of baking paper to fit.

4 When the chocolate has melted, let the bowl cool slightly then have your child carefully stir together the sticky goo.

5 Add all the other ingredients and stir again until evenly mixed and coated in chocolate. Tip into the prepared tin, push into the corners using the wooden spoon and smooth the top.

6 Cover the tin with clingfilm and leave to cool completely before putting in the refrigerator for at least 1 hour until it is set.

7 Turn out the loaf on to a chopping board and use a sharp knife and all your strength to cut into bite-sized pieces or mini bars.

Butterfly cakes

Butterfly cakes, or fairy flips as my daughter calls them, are traditional children's party fare. An easy, one-bowl mix your kids will love to make.

What to do

1. Show your child how to place a paper case in each of the cups in the patty tin while you set the oven to 180°C (350°F), Gas Mark 4.

2. Place the butter, sugar and vanilla essence in the mixing bowl and beat together with the wooden spoon or electric whisk until smooth and creamy.

3. Crack the eggs for your child and let them break them into the mixture one at a time, being careful not to let any shell fall in. Beat the mixture again between egg additions.

4. Place the sieve over the mixing bowl, sift in the flour, then stir in. Have your child drop dessertspoonfuls of the mixture into the prepared cases.

5. Bake for 20 minutes or until golden and springy to the touch.

6. Remove from the oven and allow to cool in the tin for a few minutes before transferring to a cooling rack and allowing to cool completely.

7. Meanwhile, make the butter icing. Place the ingredients in a bowl and beat together, then leave in a cool place while the cakes are cooling.

8. Using a teaspoon, dig out a circle about 2.5 cm (1 inch) in diameter from the top of each cake. Slice the cone-like piece of cake you have dug out in half.

9. Help your child fill the holes in the cakes with the icing, then gently stick the two halves of each cone back into the icing so that they stick up like a butterfly perched on top. Dust with icing sugar and/or decorate with icing pens.

Makes 12
Preparation time 20 minutes
Cooking time 20 minutes

Equipment
12 paper cake cases • 12-hole patty tin • large mixing bowl • wooden spoon or hand-held electric whisk • sieve • medium mixing bowl • cooling rack • dessertspoon • teaspoon • knife

Ingredients
100 g (3½ oz) butter or margarine, softened
100 g (3½ oz) caster sugar
2 drops vanilla essence
2 eggs
100 g (3½ oz) self-raising flour

For the icing
50 g (2 oz) butter, softened
125 g (4 oz) icing sugar, sifted
2–3 drops food colouring (optional)
1 tablespoon milk or water
icing sugar to dust
icing pens to decorate (optional)

Chocolate meringue shells

Sandwiched together with whipped chantilly cream, these are a crunchy and creamy treat.

What to do

1. Ask your child to cut out a large sheet of baking paper to fit each baking sheet while you set the oven to 150°C (300°F), Gas Mark 2.

2. Place the egg whites in the mixing bowl and help your child to whisk these until they are stiff enough that your child can hold the bowl upside down and none will fall out!

3. Add the sugar in three lots, whisking in between each addition. Then sift in the cocoa and fold in with the large metal spoon.

4. Show your child how to use the dessertspoon and a clean finger to spoon about 12 shell shapes on to each prepared baking sheet.

5. Bake for 1½ hours until crisp, then allow the meringues to cool completely on a cooling rack.

6. Meanwhile, make the chantilly cream by whipping the cream with the vanilla essence and icing sugar until stiff enough to form peaks that stay when you lift out the whisk.

7. Sandwich the meringue shells together with dessertspoonfuls of the cream and place in a pile on the serving plate.

Tiny Tip

Make sure the bowl and whisk are scrupulously clean and dry. Even the tiniest speck of oil or water will prevent the egg whites from whisking up to make a stiff and fluffy meringue.

Makes 12 complete shells
Preparation time 30 minutes
Cooking time 1½ hours

Equipment
nonstick baking paper • scissors • 2 large baking sheets • large scrupulously clean mixing bowl • hand-held electric whisk, also very clean and dry • sieve • large metal spoon • dessertspoon • cooling rack • medium mixing bowl • dessertspoon • serving plate

Ingredients
4 egg whites
175 g (6 oz) caster sugar
3 tablespoons cocoa powder

For the filling
250 ml (8 fl oz) double cream
2 drops vanilla essence
1 tablespoon icing sugar, sieved

4

Something savoury

Pizza faces

Makes 2 x 10 cm (4 inch) pizzas
Preparation time 15 minutes
Cooking time 15–20 minutes

Equipment
**large baking sheet • sieve • large mixing
bowl • wooden spoon • rolling pin**

Ingredients
few drops cooking oil for greasing
**150g (5 oz) self-raising flour, plus extra
    for dusting**
**40 g (1½ oz) butter, cold and cut into
    small pieces**
pinch of salt
3–4 tablespoons milk
1 tablespoon olive oil

For the topping
4 tablespoons passata
**strips of pepper, olives, cherry tomatoes,
    sliced mushrooms, basil leaves, ham
    slices and pineapple pieces to garnish**
**Freshly grated mozzarella cheese for
    sprinkling, plus slices for eyes if desired**

It's a strange fact but children will eat almost anything that's been made into a face. I've even seen olives pass my daughter's lips, although I'm sure she'd deny it!

What to do

1 Sprinkle a few drops of cooking oil on the baking sheet and have your child smear it all over, then wash their hands. Set the oven to 180°C (350°F), Gas Mark 4.

2 Sift the flour into a large mixing bowl, add the butter and salt and show your child how to rub the ingredients together with their fingertips until the butter is broken up and covered with flour and the mixture resembles fine breadcrumbs.

3 Add the milk and olive oil and mix with a wooden spoon, then put your hands back into the mixture and gently bring it together into a ball of soft dough.

4 Divide the dough into two and make each into a ball. Scatter some flour over the work surface and place one of the balls in the centre.

5 Using the rolling pin, help your child roll the dough out to a circle about 10 cm (4 inches) across. Then lay the circle on to the prepared baking sheet and roll out the other one.

6 Spoon 2 tablespoons of passata on to the centre of each pizza, then spread out to the edges.

7 Decorate the pizzas with the toppings. Finally sprinkle grated cheese over the top.

8 Bake for 15–20 minutes, until the edges are golden brown and the cheese melted and golden.

Bread monsters

Making bread is easy and great fun. For tiny toddlers you can make up the dough and let them play with it to their heart's content.

What to do

1 Sprinkle a few drops of cooking oil on the baking sheet and have your child smear it over with their fingers.

2 Sift the flour and salt in the mixing bowl and add the yeast, vegetable oil and water. Mix everything together with the wooden spoon, then put your hands into the bowl and draw the mixture together into a firm dough.

3 If the mixture is too dry to come together, add a little more water. If the mixture is too sticky and sticks to your hands, add some more flour.

4 Sprinkle flour over the work surface and tip the dough on to it. Have your child knead the dough by pushing, folding and turning it. You can be brutal with it: the more work, the better. Knead it for at least 5 minutes. (See tips for kneading dough on page 10.)

5 Break the dough into 8 equal pieces and knead into balls. Make a pointy snout at one end of each ball and place on the baking sheet. Leave plenty of space between the rolls as they will double in size. Help your child to make the prickles by snipping into the dough with the tips of scissors. Press halves of currants into the dough for eyes.

6 Cover the rolls with a clean tea towel, then leave in a warm place for 1 hour or until they have doubled in size.

7 Set the oven to 230°C (450°F), Gas Mark 8. Brush the rolls with the beaten egg and bake for 15–20 minutes. If the rolls are cooked they will sound hollow when tapped on the bottom (remember to pick them up with oven gloves as they will be hot). Transfer to a cooling rack.

Makes 8
Preparation time 30 minutes, plus rising
Cooking time 15–20 minutes

Equipment
large baking sheet • sieve • large mixing bowl • wooden spoon • scissors • tea towel • pastry brush • oven gloves • cooling rack

Ingredients
few drops of cooking oil for greasing
350 g (11½ oz) strong white flour, plus extra for dusting
3 g (½ a sachet) fast-action dried yeast
1 teaspoon salt
1 tablespoon vegetable oil
200 ml (7 fl oz) preboiled warm water
few currants, cut in half, to decorate
1 egg, beaten, to glaze

Cheesy feet

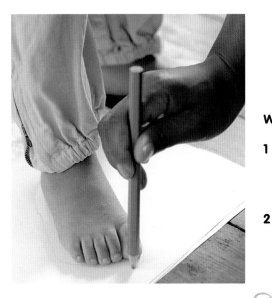

Makes about 9 feet
Preparation time 10–15 minutes
Cooking time 10 minutes

Equipment
**non-stick baking paper · scissors · large
baking sheet · foot-shaped pastry cutter
or foot template (see Tiny tip below) and
knife · oven gloves · cooling rack**

Ingredients
**plain flour, for dusting
375 g (12 oz) sheet ready-rolled puff
pastry, thawed if frozen and taken
out of the refrigerator 15 minutes
before use
50 g (2 oz) Parmesan cheese, freshly
grated
½ red pepper or a few cherry tomatoes**

Kids will love these really easy savoury biscuits
cut into feet shapes and decorated with tiny red
pepper or cherry tomato 'toenails'!

What to do

1   Set the oven to 180°C (350°F), Gas Mark 4. Cut out a
    square of non-stick baking paper to fit a large baking
    sheet and place on top of the baking sheet.

2   Sprinkle a little flour on to the work surface and remove
    the pastry from its wrapping. Carefully unroll the pastry
    until it is flat, pressing it down gently with your fingers to
    flatten any creases and mend any cracks.

 3   Show your child how to use a pastry cutter to cut out
    about 9 feet shapes. Place them spread apart on the baking
    sheet. Even very young children will be able to help with
    this. (If you do not have a foot-shaped pastry cutter, see
    Tiny Tip below for instructions on making a template. Lay
    this template on the dough and cut around it with a knife.)

4   Cut tiny pieces of the pepper or tomato with scissors.

5   Sprinkle the feet with the grated cheese, then add the
    pepper or tomato pieces – kids will really enjoy pressing
    them on to the feet as toenails.

6   Put the feet in the hot oven, making sure children stand
    well back, for 10–15 minutes or until golden brown and
    puffed up. Carefully remove them from the oven using
    oven gloves and then leave to cool on a cooling rack
    before tucking in!

Tiny Tip

To make a foot template, get your little one to stand on a piece
of card, draw around the outline of their foot and cut out.

Mini quiches

These little quiches are fun to make and can be filled with your child's favourite foods. They are great for lunch boxes and picnics too.

Makes 18
Preparation time 45 minutes
Cooking time 20 minutes

Equipment
2 x 12-hole patty tins • **8 cm (3½ inch) plain or fluted cutter** • **measuring jug** • **fork** • **small bowl** • **dessertspoon**

Ingredients
cooking oil
plain flour, for dusting
375 g (12 oz) ready-rolled shortcrust pastry, thawed if frozen and taken out of the refrigerator 15 minutes before use
2 eggs
200 ml (7 fl oz) milk
pinch of salt
4 slices ham, diced
2 spring onions, chopped
5 cherry tomatoes, chopped
50 g (2 oz) Cheddar cheese, grated

What to do

1   Set the oven to 220°C (425°F), Gas Mark 7, and sprinkle some oil into the cups of the patty tins. Ask your child to smear the oil all over the cups.

2   Sprinkle some flour on to a work surface and unroll the pastry. Have your child flatten it with the balls of their hands.

3   Show them how to stamp circles out of the pastry with the cutter and place each circle in a cup of the tin, gently pressing it down with their fingertips.

4   Place the eggs, milk and salt in a measuring jug and beat with a fork.

5   Put the ham, spring onions and cherry tomatoes into a bowl and mix together. Ask your child to put a dessertspoonful of the mixture into each pastry cup.

6   Pour some of the egg and milk mixture into each cup.

7   Sprinkle some grated cheese over the top.

8   Bake the quiches for 20 minutes or until set and golden. Eat them hot or cold.

Money bags

Filo pastry is great to paint with a pastry brush and these frilly bags are spectacular and tasty.

Makes 12
Preparation time 30 minutes
Cooking time 5–10 minutes

Equipment
**large baking sheet • 2 small bowls •
tea towel • sharp knife • pastry
brush • teaspoon**

Ingredients
**100 ml (3½ fl oz) cooking oil
100 g (3½ oz) feta cheese, chopped
   into small dice
100 g (3½ oz) cherry tomatoes,
   chopped into quarters
bunch of basil, parsley or chives,
   roughly chopped
pepper
plain flour, for dusting
250 g (8 oz) filo pastry, thawed if frozen**

What to do

1   Sprinkle a few drops of the oil on to the baking sheet and ask your little one to smear it all over with their hands while you set the oven to 190°C (375°F), Gas Mark 5.

2   Put the feta, tomatoes and herbs into a small bowl. Season with pepper and stir gently together.

3   Ask your child to sprinkle a little flour over the work surface then unroll the filo pastry on to it. Peel off 2 sheets and roll up the rest for later, keeping it moist under a damp tea towel. Place one sheet on top of the other and using a sharp knife cut both into 6 squares each measuring about 12 cm (5 inches).

4   Show your child how to brush these squares with a little oil (pour the oil into a bowl) and then stack 3 squares on top of one another so that they make a 12-pointed star.

5   Help them take a heaped teaspoon of the cheese mixture and place it in the middle of the squares.

6   Now for the tricky bit. Pick up the edges of the squares and pinch them together to make a bag. It's easy once you get the hang of it but very little ones may need help.

7   Place the parcel on the prepared baking sheet and repeat with the other squares of pastry until you have made 4 parcels. Then repeat with 2 more sheets of the pastry until you have used all the filling mixture.

8   Bake for 5–10 minutes or until crisp and golden, then remove from the oven and allow to cool on the baking sheet.

Tiny Tip

Wrap up the leftover filo pastry sheets in clingfilm and keep them in the refrigerator until next time.

Garlic puffy bread

Children love helping themselves to this lovely soft focaccia and it's surprisingly easy to make.

Makes 1 x 35 cm (14 inch) circle of bread
Preparation time 45 minutes, plus rising
Cooking time 10–15 minutes

Equipment
small mixing bowl • wooden spoon • 28 x 18 cm (11 x 7 inch) shallow baking tin • kitchen paper • large mixing bowl • clingfilm

Ingredients
225 ml preboiled warm water
2 teaspoons active dried yeast
1 teaspoon sugar
1 tablespoon olive oil
2 x 150 g (5 oz) packs pizza base mix
plain flour, for dusting
2 garlic cloves, thinly sliced
1 teaspoon salt flakes

What to do

 1 Have your child put the warm water, yeast and sugar into a small mixing bowl. Stir together, then leave in a warm place for 15 minutes or until frothy on top.

 2 Meanwhile, pour a few drips of olive oil on to the baking tin and have your little one smear it all over with their hands or a piece of kitchen paper.

3 Put the pizza base mix in a large mixing bowl and have your child add the yeast mixture and then stir it all together to make a soft dough.

4 Sprinkle some flour on to the work surface, place the dough in the middle then knead it for at least 5 minutes. Let your little one have a go at bashing it about but you will probably have to take over to knead the dough until it is elastic and smooth in texture. (See tips for kneading dough on page 10.)

5 Place the dough into the prepared baking tin and help your child to press it into the corners. Scatter over the garlic slices and the salt.

6 Smear some oil on to a piece of cling film and lay this over the top of the dough. Leave the dough in a warm place to rise for about 30 minutes or until it has doubled in height.

7 Set the oven to 220°C (425°F), Gas Mark 7. Show your child how to make dimples all over the dough by gently pressing their fingers into it. Drizzle over the remainder of the olive oil, then bake for 10–15 minutes, until golden brown.

8 Carefully remove from the oven and allow to cool for at least 5 minutes before eating.

Man-in-the-moon's scones

Makes about 14
Preparation time 15 minutes
Cooking time 12–15 minutes

Equipment

large baking sheet • sieve • large mixing bowl • wooden spoon • rolling pin • 6 cm (2½ inch) plain round or half-moon shaped cutter • pastry brush

Ingredients

few drops cooking oil for greasing
225 g (7½ oz) self-raising flour, plus extra for dusting
50 g (2 oz) cold butter, cut up into small pieces
pinch of salt
75 g (3 oz) Cheddar or your favourite cheese, grated
100 ml (3½ fl oz) milk
1 egg or 1 yolk, beaten, or milk, to glaze

Scones are very easy and quick to make. They make brilliant snacks – try these spread with cream cheese and ham or warm with butter.

What to do

1 Sprinkle a few drops of cooking oil on the baking sheet and have your child smear it all over while you set the oven to 200ºC (400ºF), Gas Mark 6.

2 Sift the flour and salt into a large mixing bowl. Add the butter and show your child how to rub the butter and flour together between their thumbs and fingers until the butter is broken up and covered with flour and the mixture resembles fine breadcrumbs.

3 Stir in 50 g (2 oz) of the cheese, add the milk and mix with a wooden spoon. Then put your hands back into the mixture and gently bring it together into a ball of soft dough.

4 Sprinkle flour on to the work surface and tip the dough into the middle. Gently roll the dough out until it is about 2.5 cm (1 inch) thick (it doesn't need much rolling).

5 Help your child use the cutter to cut out shapes and place them on the baking sheet. Brush with the beaten egg or some milk and sprinkle with the remaining cheese.

6 Bake for 12–15 minutes or until firm and golden.

Tiny Tip

To have lovely light, crumbly scones the secret is not to handle the mixture any more than you have to. It's the opposite of bread, in fact, which you need to knead.

Cheesy twists

Makes about 15
Preparation time 15 minutes
Cooking time 8–12 minutes

Equipment
non-stick baking paper • **scissors** •
2 baking sheets • **cheese grater** • **large**
mixing bowl • **sieve** • **wooden spoon** •
rolling pin • **sharp knife**

Ingredients
50 g (2 oz) Cheddar cheese
75 g (3 oz) self-raising flour, plus extra
for dusting
½ teaspoon mustard powder
50 g (2 oz) butter, cold and cut into
small pieces
1 egg

These little cheese straws were my first culinary triumph as a child.

What to do

1   Set the oven to 220°C (425°F), Gas Mark 7, and cut two pieces of baking paper to fit the two baking sheets.

2   Help your child to grate the cheese into the mixing bowl, then rest the sieve on top of the bowl, add the flour and mustard powder and show how to tap the sides or shake the sieve so the ingredients fall through.

3   Add the butter to the mix, then show your little one how to get their hands into the mixture and rub the cheese, butter and flour together between their thumbs and fingers until the butter is broken up and covered in flour and the mixture looks like fine breadcrumbs.

4   Separate the egg for your child into yolk and white. Add the yolk to the mixture and discard the white. Stir with a wooden spoon until you have a stiff dough.

5   Sprinkle lots of flour over a work surface and put the dough in the middle. Children can easily shape this dough with their hands and roll it with a floured rolling pin until it is about 5 mm (¼ inch) thick.

6   Take a sharp knife and cut the dough into long strips, about 1 cm (2½ inches) thick. Help your child to pick up each strip carefully and twist it gently before laying it on one of the prepared baking sheets.

7   Bake for 8–12 minutes until golden brown, then remove from the oven and allow to cool on the baking sheets.

Sunshine cornbread

A lovely soft, golden-yellow bread that's delicious warm or cold with butter. Great with soups, stews or cheese and pickles.

What to do

1 Set the oven to 180°C (350°F), Gas Mark 4. Let your child smear butter all over the baking tin, using their fingers or a piece of kitchen paper.

2 Have them sift the cornmeal, flour, baking powder, bicarbonate of soda and salt into a large mixing bowl and mix them together.

3 Place the yogurt, milk, maple syrup or brown sugar, eggs and melted butter into another mixing bowl and beat together with a fork or whisk.

4 Pour the dry ingredients into the wet and ask your child to stir them all together, just enough to combine them into a batter, as over-stirring can make the cornbread tough.

5 Help them to tip the mixture into the prepared tin then put it in the oven and bake for 20–25 minutes or until golden brown on top and a skewer poked into the middle comes out clean.

6 Allow to cool a little in the tin, then tip out on to a cooling rack. When cool, cut into 12 squares and serve warm or cold.

Makes 12 squares
Preparation time 15 minutes
Cooking time 20–25 minutes

Equipment

baking tin, 20 cm (8 inches) square · kitchen paper · sieve · 2 large mixing bowls · wooden or large metal spoon · fork or whisk · skewer · cooling rack · sharp knife

Ingredients

knob of butter or margarine for greasing
200 g (7 oz) cornmeal (polenta)
225 g (8 oz) plain flour
1 tablepoon baking powder
1 teaspoon bicarbonate of soda
1 teaspoon salt
425 ml (¾ pint) plain yogurt
100 ml (3½ fl oz) milk
50 ml (2 fl oz) maple syrup
   or 50 g (2 oz) brown sugar
2 eggs
50 g (2 oz) butter, melted

Courgette and cheese muffins

Delicious savoury muffins that are very quick to make and simple enough for children to do all by themselves.

What to do

1   Ask your child to place the paper cases in the muffin tin while you set the oven to 190°C (375°F), Gas Mark 5.

2   Place the courgettes and cheese in the mixing bowl, sift in the flour, bicarbonate of soda and salt and mix together.

3   Put the milk, egg and olive oil in a measuring jug and mix together with a fork. Pour this mixture into the other ingredients and stir until just mixed. Use a dessertspoon to spoon the mixture into the muffin cases so that each is nearly full.

4   Put the muffins in the preheated oven and bake for 20–25 minutes or until risen, golden and firm to the touch. Leave to cool in the tin for at least 10 minutes, then transfer to a cooling rack. Eat hot or cold.

Makes 12
Preparation time 15 minutes
Cooking time 20–25 minutes

Equipment
12 paper muffin cases • 12-cup muffin tin • large mixing bowl • sieve • wooden spoon • measuring jug • fork • dessertspoon • cooling rack

Ingredients
175 g (6 oz) courgettes, grated
200 g (7 oz) Cheddar cheese, grated
250 g (8 oz) self-raising flour
1 teaspoon bicarbonate of soda
½ teaspoon salt
200 ml (7 fl oz) milk
1 egg
4 tablespoons olive oil

5

Festive fun

Little devils' cakes

These cakes are devilishly chocolatey with little red horns.

What to do

1   Show your child how to place the paper cases in the patty tin while you set the oven to 180°C (350°F), Gas Mark 4.

2   Put the butter, sugar and vanilla essence in the mixing bowl and help your child beat them together until creamy.

3   Add the eggs and beat the mixture again, then sift in the flour and cocoa powder and stir them in. Have your child spoon the mixture into the cake cases with a dessertspoon so they are half full.

4   Bake for 10–15 minutes or until risen and firm to the touch. Remove from the oven and allow to cool for a few minutes before transferring to a cooling rack and letting cool completely.

5   Put 1½ blocks of fondant icing in a bowl, add about a tablespoon of preboiled warm water and stir until you have a thick but spreadable icing. When the cakes are cool, spread the icing over the tops with the back of a teaspoon or with a palette knife.

6   Have your child take small pieces of the remaining fondant icing and roll them into devil's horns then stick them into the wet icing on top of the cakes.

Makes 12
Preparation time 15 minutes
Cooking time 10–15 minutes

Equipment
12 paper cake cases • 12-cup patty tin • large mixing bowl • wooden spoon • sieve • dessertspoon • cooling rack • tablespoon • medium mixing bowl • palette knife or teaspoon

Ingredients
100 g (3½ oz) butter or margarine, softened
100 g (3½ oz) caster sugar
Few drops vanilla essence
2 eggs
100 g (3½ oz) self-raising flour
3 tablespoons cocoa powder
2 packs (250 g/18 oz) ready-made red fondant icing, to decorate

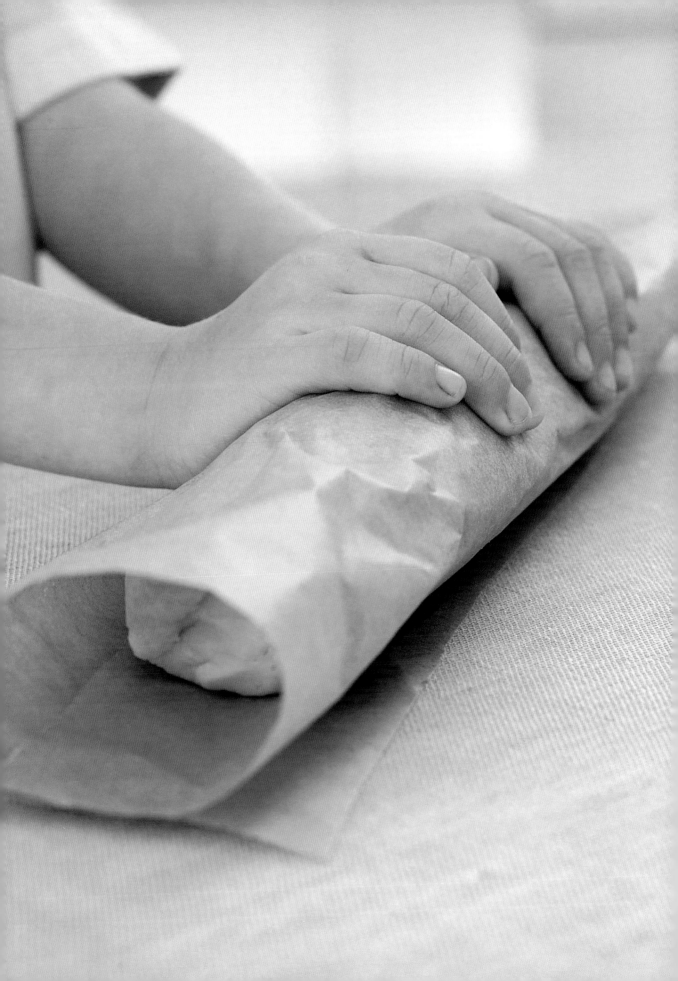

Cobweb biscuits

These scrummy cookies are what's known as refrigerator biscuits as the mixture is chilled until firm enough to slice very thinly.

Makes about 30
Preparation time 30 minutes, plus chilling
Cooking time 8–10 minutes

Equipment
large mixing bowl • **sieve** • **wooden spoons** • **clingfilm or baking paper** • **nonstick baking paper** • **scissors** • **sharp knife** • **baking sheet** • **cooling rack** • **small mixing bowl** • **teaspoon**

Ingredients
275 g (9 oz) plain flour, plus extra for dusting
200 g (7 oz) butter, cold, cut into small pieces
100 g (3½ oz) icing sugar
2 teaspoons vanilla essence

For the icing
125 g (4 oz) icing sugar
1 tablespoon preboiled warm water
black icing pen
small spider sweets or cake decorations

What to do

1. Put the butter into a large mixing bowl, sift in the flour and show your child how to rub the butter into the flour with their fingertips until the mixture resembles fine breadcrumbs. Stir in the icing sugar and vanilla essence and have your child squish the mixture together with their hands until it comes together into a ball.

2. Tip the mixture out on to a floured work surface and ask your child to squidge it together with their hands and then shape and roll it into a long sausage shape. Wrap in clingfilm or baking paper and chill for at least an hour.

3. Set the oven to 200°C (400°F), Gas Mark 6, and ask your child to cut out a sheet of nonstick baking paper to fit the baking sheet. Remove the clingfilm or baking paper from the dough and slice as thinly as possible. Place these slices on the prepared baking sheet.

4. Bake for 8–10 minutes or until the biscuits are a light golden brown. Leave to cool on the baking sheet for 5 minutes, then transfer to a cooling rack to cool completely.

5. Meanwhile, make the glacé icing by sifting the icing sugar into a bowl, then add the water and stir it in. Add more water drop by drop until you have a thick icing that coats the back of the spoon.

6. When the biscuits are cool, use a teaspoon to coat each with white icing. Then take the black icing pen and draw on a simple cobweb design. Draw or stick little spiders on to the webs, then allow to set before serving.

Pumpkin heads

Makes 12
Preparation time 30 minutes
Cooking time 10–15 minutes

Equipment
12 paper cake cases • 12-cup patty tin • large mixing bowl • wooden spoon • sieve • dessertspoon • cooling rack

Ingredients
100 g (3½ oz) butter or margarine, softened
100 g (3½ oz) caster sugar
few drops vanilla essence
2 eggs
100g (3½ oz) self-raising flour

To decorate
1 pack ready-to-roll coloured icing (contains 4 x 125 g (4 oz) packs in red, yellow, green and black)
black icing pen (optional)

Children will have great fun squishing the icing for this recipe and rolling the pumpkin heads.

What to do

 1 Show your child how to place the paper cases in the tin while you set the oven to 180°C (350°F), Gas Mark 4.

2 Put the butter, sugar and vanilla essence in the mixing bowl and help your child beat them together until creamy.

 3 Add the eggs and beat the mixture again, then sift in the flour and stir it in. Have your child spoon the mixture into the cake cases with a dessertspoon so they are half full.

4 Bake for 10–15 minutes or until risen and golden. Remove from the oven and allow to cool for a few minutes before transferring to a cooling rack and letting cool completely.

5 Take the red and the yellow icing out of their packs and ask your little one to squash them together with their hands until they are mixed to form orange.

6 Pinch off a little piece of the green icing and shape into a ball, then flatten into a circle and gently push on to the top of a cake. Pinch off a bigger piece of the orange icing and ask your child to roll it into a ball. Place this on top of the green 'pumpkin patch'. Now pinch a tiny piece of green and roll into a stalk and push on to the top of the orange pumpkin. Also take tiny pinches of the black and use to make eyes and a crooked smile. Alternatively, if your child finds it easier, draw the face on to the pumpkin head with a black icing pen.

Bonfire buns

Simple chocolate orange buns made by the easiest one-bowl, one-mixture method and decorated to look like mini bonfires.

Makes 8
Preparation time 10 minutes
Cooking time 15 minutes

Equipment
8 paper muffin cases • 8-cup muffin tin • food processor (or mixing bowl and wooden spoon) • dessertspoon • cooling rack • sharp knife • large serving plate • teaspoon

Ingredients
**100 g (3½ oz) butter, softened
100 g (3½ oz) caster sugar
2 eggs
175 g (6 oz) self-raising flour
25 g (1 oz) cocoa powder**

For the icing
**75 g (3 oz) butter, at room temperature
200 g (7 oz) icing sugar, sifted
few drops orange or yellow food colouring
2 tablespoons orange juice
2 x 150 g (5 oz) packs chocolate fingers,
  to decorate**

What to do

1   Ask your child to place 8 paper cases in the muffin tin while you set the oven to 180°C (350°F), Gas Mark 4.

2   Sift the flour and cocoa powder into a food processor, if you have one, add all other ingredients and whiz until smooth and evenly mixed. Alternatively, mash together the butter and sugar in a mixing bowl until light and creamy, beat in the eggs one at a time, then sift in the flour and cocoa powder and stir until evenly mixed.

3   Help your child to spoon the mixture into the muffin cases so that they are each just over half full.

4   Bake in the oven for 15 minutes or until risen and firm to the touch. Remove from the oven and leave to cool in the tin for 10 minutes before transferring to a cooling rack to cool completely.

5   Meanwhile, clean the food processor or mixing bowl. Add the icing ingredients and whiz for a few seconds or mash and stir until evenly mixed, smooth and creamy.

6   Show your child how to peel the papers from the cool cakes, then take each bun and slice off the part that has risen above the top of the muffin case. Slice this top part into two pieces and turn the bun upside-down on a serving plate so it sits on the cut edge.

7   Help your child to spread a coating of icing around the sides and then put a blob on the top of each bun. Stick the two pieces of sliced-off cake back on the top of each bun.

8   Show your child how to stick about 8 chocolate fingers vertically around the sides of each bun so that they look like a stack of bonfire wood.

Hot cross buns

Making your own hot cross buns together is a lovely way to spend an Easter Saturday morning.

What to do

1. Sprinkle a few drops of cooking oil on to the baking sheets and have your child smear it over with their fingers.

2. Put the flour, yeast, salt, spices and dried fruit in the mixing bowl and have your child mix them all together with their hands.

3. Add the vegetable oil and water and mix everything together with the wooden spoon. Then have your child put their hands back into the bowl and draw the mixture together into a firm dough. If the mixture is too dry to come together, add a little more water. If it is too gooey and sticks to your hands, add some more flour.

4. Sprinkle flour over the work surface and tip the dough on to it. Knead the dough for at least 5 minutes. (See tips for kneading dough on page 10.)

5. Break the dough into 10 equal-sized pieces and knead into balls, then place on the baking sheets. Leave plenty of space between the rolls as they will double in size.

6. Cover the rolls with a clean tea towel then leave in a warm place for 1 hour or until they have doubled in size.

7. Unroll the pastry and cut into strips 1 cm (½ inch) wide.

8. Have your child brush the buns with the beaten egg and then lay the pastry strips over them to form a cross. Trim the pastry and use the offcuts for the next bun until all the buns are decorated.

9. Brush the buns again with egg and bake for 15–25 minutes or until golden. Remove from the oven and leave to cool for a few minutes, then transfer to a cooling rack and allow to cool completely or eat warm.

Makes 10
Preparation time 30 minutes, plus rising
Cooking time 15–25 minutes

Equipment

2 baking sheets • **large mixing bowl** • **wooden spoon** • **tea towel** • **knife** • **pastry brush** • **cooling rack**

Ingredients

few drops of cooking oil for greasing
350 g (11½ oz) strong white flour, plus extra for dusting
3 g (½ a sachet) fast-action dried yeast
1 teaspoon salt
½ teaspoon mixed spice
1 teaspoon ground cinnamon
25 g (1 oz) mixed peel
25 g (1 oz) currants or raisins
1 tablespoon of vegetable oil
200 ml (7 fl oz) preboiled warm water
75 ml (3 fl oz) milk

To decorate

375 g (12 oz) pack ready-rolled shortcrust pastry, thawed if frozen and taken out of the refrigerator 15 minutes before use (you will only need half the pack)
1 egg, beaten

Easter nests

Wonderfully simple, little oaty nests are filled with chocolate eggs for Easter.

Makes 12
Preparation time 20 minutes
Cooking time 15 minutes

Equipment
large saucepan • **wooden spoon** •
12 paper cup cake cases • **12-cup patty tin** • **dessertspoon** • **teaspoon**

Ingredients
75 g (3 oz) butter
50 g (2 oz) soft light brown sugar
1 tablespoon golden syrup or honey
125 g (4 oz) porridge oats
mini sugar-coated chocolate eggs, to decorate

What to do

1 Set the oven to 180°C (350°F), Gas Mark 4. Show your child how to place the paper cases in the cups of the patty tin.

2 Help your child to measure out the butter, sugar and golden syrup into a large saucepan.

3 Place over a gentle heat on the hob and stir until melted together and just starting to bubble. Remove the pan from the heat and add the oats, then stir together until they are evenly covered.

4 Use a dessertspoon to spoon the mixture into the paper cases so that they are nearly full.

5 Bake in the oven for 15 minutes. Remove them from the oven for your child and leave to cool for 15 minutes, then help them to make a dip in the middle of each one with the tip of a teaspoon so that they look like little nests.

6 Leave to finish cooling. When the nests are cool, ask your child to put a few mini eggs into each one to decorate then peel off the paper cases to serve.

Easter biscuits

This dough is quick to make and then can be cut into whatever shapes you want and decorated with flair and imagination!

What to do

1   Help your child to cut 2 large sheets of baking paper to cover the baking sheets.

2   Place the butter and sugar in a large mixing bowl and help your child beat them until creamy with a wooden spoon or hand-held electric whisk.

3   Crack the egg for your child and add with the vanilla essence. Mix again until smooth.

4   Sift in the flour and stir to make a soft dough. Have your child use their hands to pull all the bits together into a ball. If the dough is very sticky, add a little more flour.

5   Wrap the dough in clingfilm and chill it for 1 hour.

6   Set the oven to 180°C (350°F), Gas Mark 4. Dust a work surface with flour and help your little one roll or press out the dough with their fingers until it is about 5mm (¼ inch) thick.

7   Show your child how to use the cutters to cut out bunnies and chicks and place them on the prepared baking sheets.

8   Bake the biscuits for 10–15 minutes or until a pale golden colour, then transfer to a cooling rack and leave to cool.

9   Make up the glacé icing by stirring the water into the icing sugar in one bowl. Tranfer half the icing to the second bowl. Adding the colouring to one bowl drop by drop. Use a teaspoon to spread the white icing over the bunnies and the yellow icing over the chicks, then decorate with cake decorations and/or icing pens.

Makes about 30
Preparation time 30 minutes, plus chilling
Cooking time 10–15 minutes

Equipment
nonstick baking paper • scissors • 2 large baking sheets • large mixing bowl • wooden spoon or hand-held electric whisk • sieve • clingfilm • rolling pin • 1 large and 1 small bunny and/or chick-shaped cutters • cooling rack • 2 small mixing bowls • dessertspoon • teaspoon

Ingredients
100 g (3½ oz) butter or margarine, softened
100 g (3½ oz) caster sugar
few drops vanilla essence
1 egg
250g (8 oz) plain flour

To decorate
250 g (8 oz) icing sugar
2 tablespoons preboiled warm water
For the chicks
yellow food colouring
small cake decorations or icing pens
For the bunnies
few white mini marshmallows or other bunny tail-like decorations

Christmas garlands

Makes 6
Preparation time 30 minutes
Cooking time 15 minutes

Equipment
**nonstick baking paper • scissors •
2 baking sheets • large mixing
bowl • wooden spoon • pastry
brush • cooling rack**

Ingredients
**50 g (2 oz) butter
150 g (5 oz) plain flour
50 g (2 oz) caster sugar, plus a little for
     sprinkling
finely grated rind of a small unwaxed
     lemon
1 egg, beaten
pieces of angelica and glacé cherries, to
     decorate**

These garlands are fun to make and very
Christmassy. Instead of eating them, they could
be hung by ribbons from your tree.

What to do

1   Help your child to cut out and line two baking sheets
    with the nonstick paper while you set the oven to 190°C
    (375°F), Gas Mark 5.

2   Put the butter in a bowl, sift in the flour and show your child
    how to rub the ingredients together between their thumbs
    and fingers until the mixture resembles fine breadcrumbs.

3   Add the sugar and lemon rind and have your little one stir
    everything together with a wooden spoon. Add most of
    the egg and stir again until the mixture comes together,
    then have them put their hands in again and draw the
    dough together into a ball.

4   Show your child how to pick off small pieces of dough
    and roll them into ball, each about the size of a cherry.
    Press 8 balls of the cookie dough together into a circle,
    then repeat to make a further 5 garlands. Place small
    pieces of glacé cherry or angelica between the balls.

5   Bake for about 15 minutes or until pale golden in colour.

6   Just before the end of the cooking time, brush with the
    remainder of the egg and sprinkle with caster sugar, then
    return to the oven to finish cooking.

7   Remove from the oven and allow to cool a little before
    transferring to a cooling rack.

Meringue snowmen

Meringues are a great favourite of ours and with an electric whisk they're a cinch to make. Children will enjoy making the snowmen shapes and giving them faces and will relish eating them.

Makes 9–12
Preparation time 20 minutes
Cooking time 1½ hours or overnight

Equipment
nonstick baking paper • scissors • 2 baking trays • small bowl • hand-held electric or hand whisk • large mixing bowl • teaspoon • tablespoon

Ingredients
3 egg whites
125 g (4 oz) caster sugar

To decorate
glacé cherries, cut into pieces
currants
mixed peel

What to do

1 Set the oven to its lowest setting and help your child cut out 2 squares of nonstick baking paper to fit the baking sheets.

2 Show your child how to separate the egg white from the yolk by cracking each egg in half over a bowl and carefully tipping the egg yolk from one half of the shell to the other while letting the white fall into the bowl below.

3 Help them to whisk the egg whites in a mixing bowl with an electric or hand whisk until the egg whites form firm peaks and you can hold the bowl upside down without the mixture falling out. Add half the sugar and briefly whisk again, then add the remaining sugar and whisk again but only enough to mix in the sugar and make a thick, glossy meringue mixture.

4 Show your child how to use a teaspoon to place a meringue head on a baking sheet and then use a tablespoon for the snowman's body. Repeat to make 9–12 snowmen. Use currants for their eyes, glacé cherry pieces for their mouths and give them buttons down their fronts with more currants or pieces of mixed peel.

5 Bake the meringues for 1 ½ hours. For best results, put them in the oven for an hour and then turn it off, leaving the meringues in there for 3–4 hours or until the oven is completely cool. This can easily be done overnight. In the morning you will have perfectly crisp meringues.

Tiny Tip

To whisk up egg whites successfully, the bowl and whisk must be scrupulously clean and dry

Rudolph's Santa snacks

We have it on good authority that Rudolph likes to make these to keep Santa going through the most important night of the year.

Makes about 14
Preparation time 15 minutes
Cooking time 15 minutes

Equipment
nonstick baking paper • **scissors** •
baking sheet • **plastic bag** • **rolling pin**
• **plate** • **large mixing bowl** •
wooden spoon • **sieve** • **cooling rack**

Ingredients
50 g (2 oz) cornflakes
100 g (3½ oz) butter or margarine,
softened
75 g (3 oz) caster sugar
1 egg yolk
few drops vanilla essence
125 g (4 oz) self-raising flour
25 g (1 oz) cornflour
7 glacé cherries, sliced in half, to
decorate

What to do

1 Set the oven to 190°C (375°F), Gas Mark 5, and help your child to cut out a piece of baking paper to fit the baking sheet.

2 Put the cornflakes in a plastic bag and have your child crush them with their hand or bash them with a rolling pin, then tip on to a plate and keep for later.

3 Put the butter and sugar into the mixing bowl and help your little one cream them together with a wooden spoon until pale and fluffy.

4 Add the egg yolk and vanilla essence and stir in. Place the sieve on the top of the bowl, add the flour and cornflour and have your child knock them through by tapping or shaking the sieve, then stir them into the mix.

5 Ask your child to wet their hands so that the mixture doesn't stick, then take walnut-sized amounts of the mixture and roll them into about 14 balls.

6 Next, roll the balls in the cornflakes until covered. Then place them on the prepared baking sheets, leaving plenty of space between each, and decorate the top of each one with half a glacé cherry.

7 Bake the biscuits for 15 minutes, or until a light golden brown, then remove from the oven and allow to cool a little before transferring to a cooling rack.

Mini gingerbread house

This house is fun to make, but very little ones will need help with the templates and with assembly.

Makes 1
Preparation time 45 minutes plus chilling
Cooking time 15 minutes

Equipment
mixing bowl • wooden spoon or hand-held electric whisk • sieve • clingfilm • nonstick baking paper • ruler • pencil • scissors • rolling pin • sharp knife • baking sheet • fish slice • small bowl • dessertspoon • piping bag

Ingredients
100 g (3½ oz) butter or margarine, softened
100 g (3½ oz) caster sugar
1 egg
few drops vanilla essence
200 g (7 oz) self-raising flour, plus extra for dusting
1 tablespoon ground ginger

To decorate
125 g (6 oz) icing sugar
1 tablespoon preboiled warm water
sweets and Christmas cake decorations
icing pens (optional)

What to do

1   Help your child to cut a large sheet of baking paper to cover the baking sheet, then follow steps 2–4 for the Gingerbread Kings and Queens on page 46. Wrap the dough in clingfilm and chill it for 1 hour.

2   Meanwhile make the templates for the houses. Take a large sheet of baking paper and draw on it one 10 x 15 cm (4 x 6 inches) rectangle, two 10 x 7.5 cm (4 x 3 inches) rectangles and two triangles, each with two sides measuring 6 cm (2½ inches) and one side measuring 5 cm (2 inches). Cut out these shapes.

3   Set the oven to 180°C (350°F), Gas Mark 4. Sprinkle the work surface with flour and roll the dough out so that it is about 5mm (¼ inch) thick. Place the templates on the dough and cut around them with a sharp knife. Transfer each piece to a baking sheet with a fish slice. Bake for 15 minutes then remove from the oven and allow to cool on the baking sheet.

4   To make the glacé icing, sift the icing sugar into a bowl then stir together with the water until you have a thick consistency.

5   Spoon the icing into a piping bag and twist the top together down to the icing, then pipe the icing on to the house.

6   Use the largest oblong biscuit as the base and use the 2 small oblongs to form a tent shape on top. Secure with lots of icing along the join (this will look like fallen snow) and allow to set. Pipe icing along the edges of the triangles and carefully insert one into each end of the tent to enclose.

7   Use more icing, or an icing pen, and sweets to decorate the house with windows and a door. Allow to set.

Index

Acknowledgements

Executive Editor: Nicola Hill
Editor: Lisa John
Executive Art Editor: Tim Pattinson
Photographer: Vanessa Davies
Props Stylist: Marianne De Vries
Home Economist: Becky Johnson
Senior Production Controller: Manjit Sihra

Huge thank yous from the author to her mum, Sally Johnson, for introducing her to the pleasures of baking and for her enduring support and to her daughter, Summer, for her enthusiastic recipe testing and tasting. Also to Marcus, Tash, Leo and Lara for all their generous help during the writing process.